Carducci Essentials: th

suè Carducci Translated in English

First Printing: 2021

ISBN: 979-8-46776-670-6

Publisher: LiteraryJoint Press, Philadelphia, PA (USA)

www.literaryjoint.com

Ordering information for U.S. and non-U.S. trade bookstores and wholesalers: special discounts are available on quantity purchases by corporations, associations, educators, and others. For details, contact the publisher at the above listed address.

Cover: Portrait of Giosuè Carducci

TO GIOSUÈ CARDUCCI

"...One who knew

To touch the lyre with no uncertain hand.

And wake its ancient chords to music new.

Forgive if only harsh strains I command

To echo thy sweet music to the few

Who fain thy lofty soul would understand,

But to thy golden tongue have not the clue.

The old Italic gods with nymph and faun

For thee repeopled mountain, wood and dale ;

'Gainst sloth and pride thy keenest shafts were drawn

Let Love and Freedom over these prevail.'

Such was thy cry : And in their radiant dawn

Must tyrants decease and superstition pale."

Emily Tribe

SAINT MARTIN'S DAY

The fog to the bare hills
soars in the thin rain,
and below the wind
howls and churns the sea;

yet through the hamlet's alleys
from the fermenting casks
goes the pungent scent of wines
to touch a soul with glee.

On the firewood, turns
the skewer crackling:
stands the hunter whistling,
on the threshold to see

in the reddening clouds
flocks of black birds,
like exiled thoughts
as in the dusk they flee.

Original text in Italian;

<u>SAN MARTINO</u>

(from "Rime Nuove," 1887)

La nebbia a gl'irti colli
piovigginando sale,
e sotto il maestrale
urla e biancheggia il mar;

ma per le vie del borgo
dal ribollir de' tini
va l'aspro odor dei vini
l'anime a rallegrar.

Gira su' ceppi accesi
lo spiedo scoppiettando:
sta il cacciator fischiando
su l'uscio a rimirar

tra le rossastre nubi
stormi d'uccelli neri,

com'esuli pensieri,
nel vespero migrar.

THE ANCIENT LAMENT

The tree you used to reach
your infant's hand out to,
the verdant pomegranate
with pretty vermilion flowers,

in the mute solitary orchard
has now just turned green
for June is restoring it
with light and warmth.

You, blossom of my own
shaken and parched tree,
you, of my vain life
ultimate and only flower,

lay in the chilly ground,
lay in the black ground;
neither can the sun gladden you
nor love awaken you again.

PIANTO ANTICO

(from "Rime Nuove", 1887)

L'albero a cui tendevi
la pargoletta mano,
il verde melograno
da' bei vermigli fior,

nel muto orto solingo
rinverdí tutto or ora
e giugno lo ristora
di luce e di calor.

Tu fior de la mia pianta
percossa e inaridita,
tu de l'inutil vita
estremo unico fior,

sei ne la terra fredda,
sei ne la terra negra;

né il sol più ti rallegra

né ti risveglia amor.

THE OX

I cherish you, oh pious Ox; a meek sensation
Of vigor and peace you bestow to my heart,
Oh, like a monument you stand, solemn
You look at the free and fecund fields,

Oh, to the yoke you contentedly kneel
Seconding the agile work of a grave man:
He urges and spurs you, and, with the slow
rolling of your patient eyes alone, you answer.

Through your wide nostril, black and wet
Your spirit fumes, and like a glad hymn
The bellow is dispersed in the serene air;

And within the glaucous, grave eye, wide and quiet,
shrouded in austere sweetness, is reflected
The green silent flat's heavenly flare.

Original text in Italian:

IL BOVE

(from "Rime Nuove," 1872)

T'amo, o pio bove; e mite un sentimento
Di vigore e di pace al cor m'infondi,
O che solenne come un monumento
Tu guardi i campi liberi e fecondi,

O che al giogo inchinandoti contento
L'agil opra de l'uom grave secondi:
Ei t'esorta e ti punge, e tu co 'l lento
Giro de' pazïenti occhi rispondi.

Da la larga narice umida e nera
Fuma il tuo spirto, e come un inno lieto
Il mugghio nel sereno aer si perde;

E del grave occhio glauco entro l'austera
Dolcezza si rispecchia ampïo e quïeto
Il divino del pian silenzio verde.

BEFORE SAINT GUIDO

The tall straight cypresses in double row
Go from San Guido down to Bolgheri;
Like giant youngsters at a race they go
Bounding to meet and look once more at me.

Straightway they knew me. "Welcome back again,"
Bending their heads to me they whispering say,
Why do you not alight ? Why not remain ?
The evening's cool, familiar the way,

Oh, sit down beneath our odorous shade,
Where breathes the Mistral wind from off the sea
We bear no resentment for your cannonade
Of stones once hurled, they wrought no injury!

We carry still the nests of nightingales:
Alas ! Wherefore run you so soon away ?
The sparrows round us still when evening pales
Circle in mazy flight. Oh, please, stay!

— Fair cypresses, sweet cypresses so dear,

True friends of better times now far from me,
How gladly would I stay with you here —
Gazing I answered — Oh ! how joyfully !

But, oh my cypresses, pray let me go;
This day is not as those, nor is my age.
To-day. . . . However can I make you know ?
I'm a celebrity and quite the rage.

I can read Latin now and even Greek,
I write and write as many volumes show,
In other qualities I am not weak ;
No more roguish, hence stones I no longer throw.

Especially at plants. — All the long file
Of tree tops with a doubtful murmur swayed
And the declining sun with pious smile
Between the green peaks its rosy hues scintillated.

Between the sun and the cypresses, it was clear,
They felt a kind pity for me;
Then instead of murmurs, words distinct I hear :
— You are a poor man, that we can well see.

We know it well, and the gathering winds told us
They enrapture men's waft,
How in your bosom eternal feuds
Burn, which nor wit nor skill of yours can soothe.

To us and to the oaks you shall confide
Your own heart's grief and all that mortal sadness.
Behold how calm, how blue is the ocean wide,
As therein sinks the sun with smiling gladness.

How full the sunset sky of birds in flight,
And how the sparrows cheer in their glee !
The nightingales will sing the livelong night:
I pray, stay, let those evil phantoms flee.

The evil phantoms, from some dark
Recess of your hearts battered by
incessant thought, flicker as in graveyards
putrid flames before the passer-by.

Oh, please, stay! To-morrow at noontide
When beneath the spreading oak-trees broad shade
The horses gather closely side by side
And all the sultry plain is in silence laid.

Hymns that ever pass between heaven and earth
We cypresses for you shall recite,
And nymphs who from the hollow elms come forth
Will come to fan you with their veils of white;

And Pan the eternal, who on the solitary height
And over the plain at this hour lonely fares,
Shall drown in heavenly harmony's delight
The dissonance, Oh mortal, of your cares. –

And I reply – Far away, beyond the Apennines
Tittì awaits for me –; let me keep going.
Much like a sparrow-nestling is Tittì,
But her no feather sports as clothing.

She must eat more than cypress berries tough,
Nor do I reap like the Manzonian strain,
A fourfold payment, for the stew.
Good-bye, my cypresses, good-bye, sweet plain! –

– Then at the churchyard what would you have us say,
Where in her grave your grandma sleeping lies ? –
They fled, and seemed a train in black array
That hasting and lamenting onward goes.

From the hill-top, along the green path
from the cemetery and through the cypresses,
Tall, solemn, dressed in black
I thought granma Lucy I saw again:

Sweet Madame Lucy, from whose lips there fell,
Beneath her silvery locks, the Tuscan speech,
Not such as the Romantics fondly tell,
The stentorelli could the learned teach.

Accents from Versilia, musical and sad,
That in my heart abide like some old strain
Of Mediaeval song, descended
Full of strength and gentleness.

Oh, granma, granma, how pretty and fair
As a little child! Tell me once more,
Tell it to this man grown wise, the old tale
Of Her seeking her own love, lost and gone!

Full seven pairs of shoes have I worn out
Of iron made, to find you once again ;
Full seven staves of iron strong and stout

Have I ground down in the journey's pain !

Full seven flask with tears I made overflow
Through seven long years of bitter tears !
You sleep, my desperate cries unheeded go,
The cock crows loud, but still you sleep.

Oh granma, how beautiful, how true
The tale is still ! it's exactly this.
Have I sought thus, nor ever found the clue,
For many, many a year in vain; perhaps here it is,

Beneath these cypresses, where I to rest
No longer hope, to dwell no longer crave:
Perhaps among those above is hid my quest,
Beside, dear granma, your lonely grave.

The locomotive wheezing sped upon its way,
While I thus wept within my heart;
And a graceful pack of foals with joyful neigh,
Pleased with the din, run as the train left.

But a grey donkey, nibbling a purple thistle,
Aloof, maintained his meditative mood:

Nor deigned to glance at the strident whistle,

But slow and stolid still he chewed and chewed.

DAVANTI A SAN GUIDO

(from "Rime Nuove," 1887)

I cipressi che a Bólgheri alti e schietti
Van da San Guido in duplice filar,
Quasi in corsa giganti giovinetti
Mi balzarono incontro e mi guardâr.

Mi riconobbero, e – Ben torni ormai –
Bisbigliaron vèr me co 'l capo chino –
Perché non scendi? perché non ristai?
Fresca è la sera e a te noto il cammino.

Oh sièditi a le nostre ombre odorate
Ove soffia dal mare il maestrale:
Ira non ti serbiam de le sassate
Tue d'una volta: oh, non facean già male!

Nidi portiamo ancor di rusignoli:
Deh perché fuggi rapido così

Le passere la sera intreccian voli
A noi d'intorno ancora. Oh resta qui!

– Bei cipressetti, cipressetti miei,
Fedeli amici d'un tempo migliore,
Oh di che cuor con voi mi resterei –
Guardando io rispondeva – oh di che cuore!

Ma, cipressetti miei, lasciatem'ire:
Or non è più quel tempo e quell'età.
Se voi sapeste!... via, non fo per dire,
Ma oggi sono una celebrità.

E so legger di greco e di latino,
E scrivo e scrivo, e ho molte altre virtù;
Non son più, cipressetti, un birichino,
E sassi in specie non ne tiro più.

E massime a le piante. – Un mormorio
Pe' dubitanti vertici ondeggiò,
E il dì cadente con un ghigno pio
Tra i verdi cupi roseo brillò.

Intesi allora che i cipressi e il sole

Una gentil pietade avean di me,
E presto il mormorio si fe' parole:
– Ben lo sappiamo: un pover uomo tu se'.

Ben lo sappiamo, e il vento ce lo disse
Che rapisce de gli uomini i sospir,
Come dentro al tuo petto eterne risse
Ardon che tu né sai né puoi lenir.

A le querce ed a noi qui puoi contare
L'umana tua tristezza e il vostro duol;
Vedi come pacato e azzurro è il mare,
Come ridente a lui discende il sol!

E come questo occaso è pien di voli,
Com'è allegro de' passeri il garrire!
A notte canteranno i rusignoli:
Rimanti, e i rei fantasmi oh non seguire;

I rei fantasmi che da' fondi neri
De i cuor vostri battuti dal pensier
Guizzan come da i vostri cimiteri
Putride fiamme innanzi al passegger.

Rimanti; e noi, dimani, a mezzo il giorno,
Che de le grandi querce a l'ombra stan
Ammusando i cavalli e intorno intorno
Tutto è silenzio ne l'ardente pian,

Ti canteremo noi cipressi i cori
Che vanno eterni fra la terra e il cielo:
Da quegli olmi le ninfe usciran fuori
Te ventilando co 'l lor bianco velo;

E Pan l'eterno che su l'erme alture
A quell'ora e ne i pian solingo va
Il dissidio, o mortal, de le tue cure
Ne la diva armonia sommergerà. –

Ed io – Lontano, oltre Appennin, m'aspetta
La Tittì – rispondea -; lasciatem'ire.
È la Tittì come una passeretta,
Ma non ha penne per il suo vestire.

E mangia altro che bacche di cipresso;
Né io sono per anche un manzoniano
Che tiri quattro paghe per il lesso.
Addio, cipressi! addio, dolce mio piano! –

– Che vuoi che diciam dunque al cimitero
Dove la nonna tua sepolta sta? –
E fuggìano, e pareano un corteo nero
Che brontolando in fretta in fretta va.

Di cima al poggio allor, dal cimitero,
Giù de' cipressi per la verde via,
Alta, solenne, vestita di nero
Parvemi riveder nonna Lucia:

La signora Lucia, da la cui bocca,
Tra l'ondeggiar de i candidi capelli,
La favella toscana, ch'è sì sciocca
Nel manzonismo de gli stenterelli,

Canora discendea, co 'l mesto accento
De la Versilia che nel cuor mi sta,
Come da un sirventese del trecento,
Piena di forza e di soavità.

O nonna, o nonna! deh com'era bella
Quand'ero bimbo! ditemela ancor,
Ditela a quest'uom savio la novella

Di lei che cerca il suo perduto amor!

– Sette paia di scarpe ho consumate
Di tutto ferro per te ritrovare:
Sette verghe di ferro ho logorate
Per appoggiarmi nel fatale andare:

Sette fiasche di lacrime ho colmate,
Sette lunghi anni, di lacrime amare:
Tu dormi a le mie grida disperate,
E il gallo canta, e non ti vuoi svegliare.

– Deh come bella, o nonna, e come vera
È la novella ancor! Proprio così.
E quello che cercai mattina e sera
Tanti e tanti anni in vano, è forse qui,

Sotto questi cipressi, ove non spero,
Ove non penso di posarmi più:
Forse, nonna, è nel vostro cimitero
Tra quegli altri cipressi ermo là su.

Ansimando fuggìa la vaporiera
Mentr'io così piangeva entro il mio cuore;

E di polledri una leggiadra schiera
Annitrendo correa lieta al rumore.

Ma un asin bigio, rosicchiando un cardo
Rosso e turchino, non si scomodò:
Tutto quel chiasso ei non degnò d'un guardo
E a brucar serio e lento seguitò.

NOSTALGIA

Here's blue in between the clouds
Prevailing, dark and humid:
It ascends towards the Apennines
The rumbling storm.

Oh, could the gentle whirlwind
Carry me all the way
On its kite-like wing
To the dear Tuscan place!

Not the face or soul of friends
or relatives is inviting me there:
All who smiled at me as a child
Now are either sage or dead.

Not a desire for olive trees
Or grapevines are calling me:
I'd flee from the merry acclivities
Blessed with uberty.

From my town's vaunts

And the usual songs
I'd flee old ladies' chattering
Over marmoreal balconies!

Where the woods scarcely offer shade
To the malign crevices, and in the dusky
Plain bristling with cork trees,
The horses wander all around.

Where my sad springtime bloomed,
There in the Maremma,
Flows the stream of my thoughts
With the thunders and the storm:

There, in the black sky hovering
My country again to see,
Then with the thunder sinking
Between those hills and in that sea.

NOSTALGIA

(from "Rime Nuove," 1906)

Tra le nubi ecco il turchino
cupo ed umido prevale:
sale verso l'Apennino
brontolando il temporale.

Oh se il turbine cortese
sovra l'ala aquilonar
mi volesse al bel paese
di Toscana trasportar!

Non d'amici o di parenti
là m'invita il cuore e il volto:
chi m'arrise a i dì ridenti
ora è savio od è sepolto.

Né di viti né d'ulivi
bel desio mi chiama là:

fuggirei da' lieti clivi
benedetti d'ubertà.

De le mie cittadi i vanti
e le solite canzoni
fuggirei: vecchie ciancianti
a marmorei balconi!

Dove raro ombreggia il bosco
le maligne crete, e al pian
di rei sugheri irto e fosco
i cavalli errando van.

Là in maremma ove fiorío
la mia triste primavera,
là rivola il pensier mio
con i tuoni e la bufera:

Là nel ciel nero librarmi
la mia patria a riguardar,
poi co 'l tuon vo' sprofondarmi
tra quei colli ed in quel mar.

SONG OF MAY

May awakens the nests,
May awakens the hearts;
Brings the nettles and the flowers,
The snakes and the nightingale.

The children are cackling
On earth, the birds in the sky:
In their hair the women carry
Roses, in their eyes the sun.

Between hills, fields, and mountains
All is a weave of flowers:
They Sing sprout and love
The waters, the earth, and the sky.

And within my heart is germinating
A nice grove of thorn;
Three vipers are in my chest
And an owl within my brain.

MAGGIOLATA

(from "Rime Nuove", 1887)

Maggio risveglia i nidi,
Maggio risveglia i cuori;
Porta le ortiche e i fiori,
I serpi e l'usignol.

Schiamazzano i fanciulli
In terra, e in ciel li augelli:
Le donne han ne i capelli
Rose, ne gli occhi il sol.

Tra colli prati e monti
Di fior tutto è una trama:
Canta germoglia ed ama
L'acqua la terra il ciel.

E a me germoglia in cuore
Di spine un bel boschetto;

Tre vipere ho nel petto
E un gufo entro il cervel.

WINTER ENNUI

Was there, then, one day
The sun on this earth?
Were there roses and violets,
Light, smile, ardor?

Was there, then, one day
The sweet youth,
The glory and the beauty,
Faith, virtue, love?

That happened perhaps in the times
Of Homer and of Valmiki:
But those are ancient times,
The sun now is no longer here.

And this fog I wrap myself up with,
Fog of filthy winter
Is the ash of a world
That once was, perhaps.

TEDIO INVERNALE

(from "Rime Nuove", 1887)

Ma ci fu dunque un giorno
Su questa terra il sole?
Ci fur rose e vïole,
Luce, sorriso, ardor?

Ma ci fu dunque un giorno
La dolce giovinezza,
La gloria e la bellezza,
Fede, virtude, amor?

Ciò forse avvenne a i tempi
D'Omero e di Valmichi:
Ma quei son tempi antichi,
Il sole or non è piú.

E questa ov'io m'avvolgo
Nebbia di verno immondo

È il cenere d'un mondo
Che forse un giorno fu.

TO A BOTTLE OF 1848 VALTELLINA WINE

And you hung, vine shoot, from the Rhaetian
steeps, the flourishing scent dwelt in the murmur
of blue rivers descending the high peaks
like a run-away silvery froth,

when April of Italian glory
cheered from river Po to mount Stelvio
and the Latin people girded
Austria like a knight's belt.

And you seethed in the vat turbidly
as in a prison, when the Italian October
spasm throbbed and in the city of Chiavenna,
oh mighty Rhaetia! lined up in Vercea

sixty men still thirsty for freedom
and ready to die: Hainau contained
the bitter spirits and the Istrian horses
bristled before the three colors.

Rhaetia, to Health! your forefathers were free,

oh daughter, and you are freer in new glories!
Under the good sun of the Alps, how pleasant
it is to pour your noble wine, singing:

singing the chants of the Italian days,
when at your steps all the peoples ran,
and shone in the glaciers our
flag over the Austrian retreat.

To the known chants faint shadows rise:
those who fell yearning for victory?
Be glory, oh brothers! Not even,
the work of the century, not even, is full.

Yet in the elders dwells your soul,
your blood is fervent in the young:
oh Italy, we'll carry your flag
gloriously in the alpine winds.

A UNA BOTTIGLIA DI VALTELLINA DEL 1848

(from "Odi Barbare", 1888)

E tu pendevi tralcio da i retici
balzi odorando florido al murmure
de' fiumi da l'alpe volgenti
ceruli in fuga spume d'argento,

quando l'aprile d'itala gloria
da 'l Po rideva fino a lo Stelvio
e il popol latino si cinse
su l'Austria cingol di cavaliere.

E tu nel tino bollivi torbido
prigione, quando d'italo spasimo
ottobre fremeva e Chiavenna,
oh Rezia forte!, schierò a Vercea

sessanta ancora di morte libera
petti assetati: Hainau gli aspri animi

contenne e i cavalli de l'Istro
ispidi in vista dei tre colori.

Rezia, salute! di padri liberi
figlia ed a nuove glorie più libera!
È bello al bel sole de l'alpi
mescere il nobil tuo vin cantando:

cantando i canti de i giorni italici,
quando a' tuoi passi correano i popoli,
splendea tra le nevi la nostra
bandiera sopra l'austriaca fuga.

A i noti canti lievi ombre sorgono
quei che anelando vittoria caddero?
Sia gloria, o fratelli! Non anche,
l'opra del secol non anche è piena.

Ma nei vegliardi vige il vostro animo,
il sangue vostro ferve ne i giovani:
o Italia, daremo il altre alpi
inclita a i venti la tua bandiera.

EASTER EVE

What a song of renewed youth, of bright days of joy,
all over the clear blue sky of April
sing the church bells, with waves of soaring sounds
from the town towards hills, green in the distance!
From the defeated inferno, the crest of victory redeemed,
pure, radiant, Christ rises to heaven:
unfolding from winter the new year, and at its bloom
already forbodes the harvesting season with glee.
A new guest in this world, it's twenty years today, Mary,
since you appeared; and your first wailing
was welcomed by the sound of the loose bells singing to glory:
now you stand in the glory of the finest age,
stand like one of these forthcoming saplings of April
in the sweet breeze yield the white-rosy flower.
Oh, may the well-wishing sound of the church bells wrap
around your young head in this day of Spring and Easter too!
dispel Winter and the cold, dispel the sad hatred and the sloth,
dispel all forms of discordant life!

SABATO SANTO

(from "Rime e ritmi", 1898)

Che giovinezza nova, che lucidi giorni di gioia
per la cerula effusa chiarità de l'aprile
cantano le campane con onde e volate di suoni
da la città su' poggi lontanamente verdi!
Da i superati inferni, redimito il crin di vittoria,
candido, radïante, Cristo risorge al cielo:
svolgesi da l'inverno il novello anno, e al suo fiore
già in presagio la messe già la vendemmia ride.
Ospite nova al mondo, son oggi vent'anni, Maria,
tu t'affacciasti; e i primi tuoi vagiti coverse
doppio il suon de le sciolte campane sonanti a la gloria:
ora e tu ne la gloria de l'età bella stai,
stai com'uno di questi arboscelli schietti d'aprile
che a l'aura dolce danno il bianco roseo fiore.
Volgasi intorno al capo tuo giovin, deh, l'augure suono
de le campane anc'oggi di primavera e pasqua!
cacci il verno ed il freddo, cacci l'odio tristo e l'accidia,
cacci tutte le forme de la discorde vita!

ALPINE MIDDAY

In the great circle of the Alps, on the granite,
Bleak and faded, on candid glaciers,
Serene, intense and infinite,
Reigns the great silence of midday.

Pines trees and fir trees, in the motionless air,
Stand high under the sun that penetrates through them,
You only hear fluttering, like the sound of a zither,
The water that tenuously through the stones glided by.

Original text in Italian:

MEZZOGIORNO ALPINO

(from "Rime e Ritmi", 1899)

Nel gran cerchio de l'alpi, su 'I granito
Squallido e scialbo, su' ghiacciai candenti,
Regna sereno intenso ed infinito
Nel suo grande silenzio il mezzodí.

Pini ed abeti senza aura di venti
Si drizzano nel sol che gli penètra,
Sola garrisce in picciol suon di cetra
L'acqua che tenue tra i sassi fluí.

BY THE SEA

Tyrrhenian, my chest too is a deep sea,
And in storms, oh great one, yields not to you:
My soul roars in the waves, and around
Its short shores and the tiny sky wounds.

Shrouded in filthy foams, even in the deep,
Clashes the sand: and here and there you see
Some dumb and dirty cetacean
Gasping straight behind its dirty prey.

He contemplates the object of its algid lookouts
And points to them and count them one by one
Where beasts and sands, in vain, are furious:

Just like on this solitary dune
Your black ire and the autumnal winds
Are illuminated by the moon, useless lamp.

IN RIVA AL MARE

(from "Rime Nuove", 1887)

Tirreno, anche il mio petto è un mar profondo,
E di tempeste, o grande, a te non cede:
L'anima mia rugge ne' flutti, e a tondo
Suoi brevi lidi e il picciol cielo fiede.

Tra le sucide schiume anche dal fondo
Stride la rena: e qua e là si vede
Qualche cetaceo stupido ed immondo
Boccheggiar ritto dietro immonde prede.

La ragion de le sue vedette algenti
Contempla e addita e conta ad una ad una
Onde belve ed arene invan furenti:

Come su questa solitaria duna
L'ire tue negre e gli autunnali venti
Inutil lampa illumina la luna.

SNOWFALL

Slowly flake by flake, from a sky the colour of ashes,
Flutters the snow; no cry of life from the city rise up,

Not the call of the vendor of herbs, nor the rumble of
carts, not the songs joyous with love and youth.

Hoarsely hours moan from the square's tower, sighing through
the air as if from a world far off.

At my misted window wandering birds are tapping:
ghosts of friends returning, looking on me, calling me.

Oh, indomitable heart, be calm soon, oh, dear ones,
Soon shall I descend to silence, soon in the shadow rest.

NEVICATA

(From "Odi Barbare", 1889)

Lenta fiocca la neve pe 'l cielo cinereo: gridi,
suoni di vita più non salgono da la città,

non d'erbaiola il grido o corrente rumore di carro,
non d'amor la canzon ilare e di gioventù.

Da la torre di piazza roche per l'aere le ore
gemon, come sospir d'un mondo lungi dal dì.

Picchiano uccelli raminghi a' vetri appannati: gli amici
spiriti reduci son, guardano e chiamano a me.

In breve, o cari, in breve – tu càlmati, indomito cuore –
giù al silenzio verrò, ne l'ombra riposerò.

VIRGIL

As when the gentle moon low in the sky
Over the parched fields cool summer dew distils,
The river in the pale light gleaming fills
Its shallow banks as it glides murmuring by;

The secretive nightingale from leafy trees
Floods the vast calm with his melodious trills,
The wanderer listens, time forgets, as thrills
With thoughts of fair locks loved his memory;

And bereaved mothers who have grieved in vain,
Turn from a grave toward brightening heaven their eyes
And soothe their souls in the spreading shine;

Meanwhile the mountains and the distant sea smile,
And through tall trees the cool wind softly sighs,
Such is thy verse to me, Poet divine.

Original text in Italian:

VIRGILIO

(From "Rime Nuove", 1870)

Come, quando su' campi arsi la pia
Luna imminente il gelo estivo infonde,
Mormora al bianco lume il rio tra via
Riscintillando tra le brevi sponde;

E il secreto usignuolo entro le fronde
Empie il vasto seren di melodia,
Ascolta il viatore ed a le bionde
Chiome che amò ripensa, e il tempo oblia;

Ed orba madre, che doleasi in vano,
Da un avel gli occhi al ciel lucente gira
E in quel diffuso albor l'animo queta;

Ridono in tanto i monti e il mar lontano,
Tra i grandi arbor la fresca aura sospira:
Tale il tuo verso a me, divin poeta.

FIESOLE

Where Fiesole from her citadel saw
The livid Arno stagnate, the place
Where is now blooming Sulla's city, slow of pace,
Recalls the Franciscans, by clanging bell.

Upon the Etruscan walls, now ruined,
The lizard watches with fixed eye,
And a cypress grove, wind-wearied,
Howls, and the solitary evening shines.

From the lunate hill down to the plain
The joyous belfry dominates, as when Italians rose
In the dread year their glories to restore.

Nature dwells in your marble, Oh Mino,
In the curl-crowned boys she glows,
Maiden and mother smiling evermore.

FIESOLE

(From "Rime Nuove", 1887)

Su l'arce onde mirò Fiesole al basso,
Dov'or s'infiora la città di Silla,
Stagnar livido l'Arno, a lento passo
Richiama i francescani un suon di squilla.

Su le mura, dal rotto etrusco sasso
La lucertola figge la pupilla,
E un bosco di cipressi a i venti lasso
Ulula, e il vespro solitario brilla.

Ma dal clivo lunato a la pianura
Il campanil domina allegro, come
La risorta nel mille itala gente.

O Mino, e nel tuo marmo è la natura
Che de' fanciulli a le ricciute chiome
Ride, vergine e madre eternamente.

ST. MARY OF THE ANGELS

Oh brother Francis, how much open air
Vignola's noble dome can embrace!
Where, arms crossed, wrestling with life's ultimate pain,
Naked on the bare earth you lay.

Hot is July and over the labouring plain
rises love's canticle. Oh may the Umbrian
Song give me some trace of your strain,
And the Umbrian sky some of your glance!

On the horizon of that hill-girt land,
Its splendour softened by the mountain haze,
As if to your Heaven it were the portal,

With outstretched arms may I behold you stand,
Singing to God — Oh Lord, to Thee be praise
For Death, sweet sister of our body mortal !

Original text in Italian:

SANTA MARIA DEGLI ANGELI

(From "Rime Nuove", 1886)

Frate Francesco, quanto d'aere abbraccia
Questa cupola bella del Vignola
Dove incrociando a l'agonia le braccia
Nudo giacesti su la terra sola!

E luglio ferve e il canto d'amor vola
Nel pian laborïoso. Oh che una traccia
Diami il canto umbro de la tua parola,
L'umbro cielo mi dia de la tua faccia!

Su l'orizzonte del montan paese,
Nel mite solitario alto splendore,
Qual del tuo paradiso in su le porte,

Ti vegga io dritto con le braccia tese
Cantando a Dio — Laudato sia, signore,
Per nostra corporal sorella morte!

CROSSING THE TUSCAN MAREMMA

Sweet countryside, from you I derived
My proud demeanor and my song of disdain,
And my breast, where love and hate never subside,
How leaps my heart, as I behold you again!

How well I recognize your familiar forms,
With eyes uncertain between tears or laughter,
In those I follow the footsteps of my dreaming visions
Straying in the pursuit of the enchantment of youth.

Oh what I loved and dreamt, how vain was it!
Ever I ran, but never reached the goal;
To-morrow I shall fall; from a distance yet

The hills of yours speak peace unto the soul
With the mists that fade away and the verdant plain
that in the morning showers smiles.

Original text in Italian:

TRAVERSANDO LA MAREMMA TOSCANA

(From "Rime Nuove", 1885)

Dolce paese, onde portai conforme
l'abito fiero e lo sdegnoso canto
e il petto ov'odio e amor mai non s'addorme,
pur ti riveggo, e il cor mi balza in tanto.

Ben riconosco in te le usate forme
con gli occhi incerti tra 'l sorriso e il pianto,
e in quelle seguo de' miei sogni l'orme
erranti dietro il giovenile incanto.

Oh, quel che amai, quel che sognai, fu in vano;
e sempre corsi, e mai non giunsi il fine;
e dimani cadrò. Ma di lontano

pace dicono al cuor le tue colline
con le nebbie sfumanti e il verde piano
ridente ne le pioggie mattutine.

A MAY NIGHT

Never was the night more serene
Greeted by the vague stars
Ashore of tides and shiny weaves;
And the ancient, errant, solitary moon
Flickered on the dewy leafage,
Breaking the shadows than ran down the hills.

Candid, truthful, austere moon:
Behold the vapor and the warmth
That were rising to you from the bosky hills!
It seemed as if the nymphs awakened in the green
To compete with the virginal stars
And a sweet whisper was in the waves.

Never such an oblivious sailing through the waters
Befall any lovers beneath the moon,
As the one I, disaffected, had in the lovely green;
It was such that mighty shiny night
That it seemed to me that from the graves and the stars
Friendly ghosts came wandering on the hills.

Behold in Heaven the passing of the stars,
Ye who, asleep in the motherly hills,
from the humble graves by the sea,
beneath the fixed rays of the moon,
I saw again peopling the silent night,
Go lightly gliding over the yielding green.

Alas! How much of my green youth,
I lived again on the top of the illuminated hills,
And below, the conquered night fled again!
Then I saw some shape - forming towards me
On the waves, sketched in the moonlight -
Through her laughing eyes shone the rays of the stars.

"Remember me" she said. Then the stars
Were veiled and shadows spread athwart the green,
Suddenly in the heavens sank the moon,
And shrilly chants re-echoed through the hills,
And left alone beside the feeble waves
I felt as from a tomb grow chill the night.

When Heaven at night is thickest with stars
I joy beside the waves, stretched on the green,
To watch the moon descend behind the hills.

NOTTE DI MAGGIO

(From "Rime Nuove", 1906)

Non mai seren di piú tranquilla notte
Fu salutato da le vaghe stelle
In riva di correnti e lucid'onde;
E tremolava rorida su 'l verde,
Rompendo l'ombre che scendean da'colli,
L'antica, errante, solitaria luna.

Candida, vereconda, austera luna:
Che vapori e tepor per l'alta notte
Salíano a te da gli arborati colli!
Parea che in gara a le virginee stelle
Si svegliasser le ninfe in mezzo il verde,
E un soave sussurro era ne l'onde.

Non tale un navigar d'oblio per l'onde
Ebbero amanti mai sotto la luna,
Qual io disamorato entro il bel verde:

Che solo ai buoni splender quella notte
Pareami, e da gli avelli e da le stelle
Spirti amici vagar vidi su i colli.

O voi dormenti ne i materni colli,
E voi d'umili tombe a presso l'onde
Guardanti in cielo trapassar le stelle;
Voi sotto il fiso raggio de la luna
Rividi io popolar la cheta notte,
Lievi strisciando su 'l commosso verde.

Deh, quanta parte de l'età mia verde,
Rivissi in cima ai luminosi colli,
E vinta al basso rifuggía la notte!
Quando una forma verso me su l'onde,
Disegnata nel lume de la luna,
Vidi, e per gli occhi le ridean le stelle.

Ricordati: mi disse. Allor le stelle
Furon velate, e corse ombra su 'l verde,
E di súbito in ciel tacque la luna;
Acuti lai suonarono pe' colli;
Ed io soletto su le flebili onde
Di sepolcro sentii fredda la notte.

Quando la notte è fitta piú di stelle,

A me giova appo l'onde entro il bel verde

Mirar su i colli la sedente luna.

GEOFFREY RUDEL

Translation by EMILY A. TRIBE

From Lebanon the cool fresh morn
Sheds rosy tremors on the sea;
By Latin barque the cross is borne
From Cyprus sailing gallantly.
On deck stands Rudel, Prince of Blaye,
With fever faint, his yearning eyes
Seek on the heights above the bay
Where Tripoli's fair castle lies.

When he beholds the Asian strand.
The famous song he sings anew.
Love hath for you from far-off land
Filled all my heart with aching pain."
The drclings of the grey sea-mew
Follow the lover's sweet complaint;
On the white sails the sun grows faint,
Obscured by clouds in fleecy train.

The ship in the calm haven drops

Her anchor fast; Bertrand descends
In anxious care, naught heeds, nor stops.

Toward the hill his way he wends.
With mourning trappings all bedight
The shield of Blaye is in his hand.
He hastens to the Castle height :
"Where is the Lady Milisande"

"The messenger of love I come,
I come the messenger of death.
I come to seek you in your home
From Blaye's good lord, Geoffrey Rudel.
He caught your fame on Rumour's breath.
Unseen he loved you, sang of you.
He comes, he dies ; this poet true.
Lady, to you sends his farewell."

With pensive mien the lady rose,
Looked at the sqmre, some moments stayed,
Then a black veil around her throws,
Her face and star-like eyes to shade.
Sir Squire," quoth she, her words come fast.
Let us go where Sir Geoffrey lies.

That we may bear the first and last
Word love may utter ere he dies."

Beneath his fair tent pitched along
Beside the sea Sir Geoffrey lay.
In low tones sang one tender song
That told his heart's supreme desire.
"Lord, who didst will that far away
My love should dwell in Eastern lands,
Grant that I may in her dear hands
Commit my soul as I expire."

Guided by faithful Bertrand's hand
The lady came, the last note caught.
Before the entrance Milisande
Lingered, her heart with pity fraught.
But soon with trembling hand she threw
Her veil aside, her face left clear.
Near to her lover sad she drew.
And murmured : "Geoffrey, I am here."

Stretched on a low divan he lay,
Turning, then vainly strove to rise ;
With a long sigh the Lord of Blaye

Upon those lovely features gazed.
"Is that the face, are these the eyes
Love promised one day should be mine ?
Around that brow did I entwine
Vague dreams my waking thought had raised ?"

Just as the moon on some May night
Bursts through the clouds' encircling gloom.
Flooding the earth with silvery light,
Fills it with growth and with perfume.
So to the enchanted lover seems
This tranquil beauty to impart
Sweetness divine beyond all dreams,
Filling the dying poet's heart.

"Lady, what is this life of ours?
The fleeting shadow of a dream.
Now end the fable's transient hours,
This only love that knows not death.
To one in agony supreme
Open thine arms. On the last day
I wait for thee; a kiss now may
Commend to thee my latest breath."

The lady held him to her breast.
And bending o'er her lover pale
Upon his quivering lips she pressed
Love's kiss of greeting and farewell.
The sun broke through his misty veil.
From sky sererte shone on the sea.
The lady's golden locks set free
Like light o'er the dead poet fell.

JAUFRÈ RUDEL

(From "Poesia antica e moderna", 1880)

Dal Libano trema e rosseggia
Su 'l mare la fresca mattina:
Da Cipri avanzando veleggia
 La nave crociata latina.
A poppa di febbre anelante
Sta il prence di Blaia, Rudello,
E cerca co 'l guardo natante
Di Tripoli in alto il castello.

In vista a la spiaggia asïana
Risuona la nota canzone:
«Amore di terra lontana,
Per voi tutto il core mi duol.»
Il volo d'un grigio alcïone
Prosegue la dolce querela,
E sovra la candida vela
S'affligge di nuvoli il sol.

La nave ammaina, posando
Nel placido porto. Discende
Soletto e pensoso Bertrando,
La via per al colle egli prende.
Velata di funebre benda
Lo scudo di Blaia ha con sé:
Affretta al castel: - Melisenda
Contessa di Tripoli ov'è?

Io vengo messaggio d'amore,
Io vengo messaggio di morte:
Messaggio vengo io del signore
Di Blaia, Giaufredo Rudel.
Notizie di voi gli fûr porte,
V'amò vi cantò non veduta:
Ei viene e si muor. Vi saluta,
Signora, il poeta fedel.

La dama guardò lo scudiero
A lungo, pensosa in sembianti:
Poi surse, adombrò d'un vel nero
La faccia con gli occhi stellanti:
Scudier, - disse rapida - andiamo.

Ov'è che Giaufredo si muore?
Il primo al fedele rechiamo
E l'ultimo motto d'amore.

Giacea sotto un bel padiglione
Giaufredo al conspetto del mare:
In nota gentil di canzone
Levava il supremo desir.
Signor che volesti creare
Per me questo amore lontano,
Deh fa che a la dolce sua mano
Commetta l'estremo respir!

Intanto co 'l fido Bertrando
Veniva la donna invocata;
E l'ultima nota ascoltando
Pietosa risté su l'entrata:
Ma presto, con mano tremante
Il velo gittando, scoprì
La faccia; ed al misero amante
Giaufredo, - ella disse - son qui.

Voltossi, levossi co 'l petto
Su i folti tappeti il signore,

E fiso al bellissimo aspetto
Con lungo sospiro guardò.
Son questi i begli occhi che amore
Pensando promisemi un giorno?
È questa la fronte ove intorno
Il vago mio sogno volò?

Sí come a la notte di maggio
La luna da i nuvoli fuora
Diffonde il suo candido raggio
Su 'l mondo che vegeta e odora,
Tal quella serena bellezza
Apparve al rapito amatore,
Un'altra divina dolcezza
Stillando al morente nel cuore.

Contessa, che è mai la vita?
È l'ombra d'un sogno fuggente.
La favola breve è finita,
 Il vero immortale è l'amor.
Aprite le braccia al dolente.

Vi aspetto al novissimo bando.
Ed or, Melisenda, accomando

A un bacio lo spirto che muor.

La donna su 'l pallido amante
Chinossi recandolo al seno,
Tre volte la bocca tremante
Co 'l bacio d'amore baciò,
E il sole da 'l cielo sereno
Calando ridente ne l'onda
L'effusa di lei chioma bionda
Su 'l morto poeta irraggiò.

THE SONG OF LEGNANO

Translation by EMILY A. TRIBE

I

In Como bides the Emperor Frederick.
A messenger to Milan rides full speed.
The New Gate * enters, nor draws rein but cries :
"Oh, men of Milan, give me escort due
To Sor Gherardo,' consul of your town ! "
The consul stood in middle of the square,
The messenger bent o'er his saddle bow.
Whispered brief words and spurred him on his way.
Consul Gherardo straightway gave the sign
And trumpet blasts convened the Parliament.

II

'Twas blast of trumpet called the Parliament,
Because the palace had not risen anew
On tall pilasters, rostrum was there none.
No tower was there, no bell swung from its crown,
Among the blackened ruins, where now thorns
Grew green among low cabins built of wood.
There in the narrow public place the men
Of Milan held their Parliament, beneath
The sun of May ; from windows and from doors
The women and the children waiting watched.

III

The consul speaks : " My lords of Milan, hear !
With spring in blossom come the German hordes.
As is their wont ; their Easter feast consumed
In their own lairs, the greedy boors descend
Upon our valleys ; through the Engadine
Two excommunicate archbishops lead.
The fsur-haired Empress to her lord hath brought
Besides a faithful heart an army new ;
Como holds with the strong and leaves the league ' ;
" Down, shout the people, Down with Como, down I

IV

"My lords of Milan," says the consul, hear
In Como Frederick musters troops and goes
To join the false Pavians and the lord
Of Monferrato. Men of Milan, choose ;

Or will ye from your ramparts new await
And watch in arms, or to the Caesar send
Your messengers, or seek with spear and sword
The Barbarossa in his camp ? " We'll seek
With sword and spear," shouted the Parliament,
" With spear and sword the red-beard in his camp ! "

V

Now Albert of Giussano forward steps.
By head and shoulders he o'ertops the rest
Of those who round the consul crowd, his form
Amid the parliament rose like a tower
Stalwart and tall ; his helmet in his hand
He holds, around his brawny neck and on
His square-set shoulders broad his long dark locks
Fell free ; upon his frank and open face
The sun beats sparkling in his eye and hair ;
His voice is like the thunder heard in May.

VI

"O men of Milan, brothers, people mine.
Do ye remember those March Kalends ? "
Says Albert of Giussano, To Lodi rode
Your wan-faced consuls, who with naked swords
Upheld in hand unto the Emperor swore
Obedience. Three hundred strong we rode.
On the fourth day we laid down at his feet
Our thirty-six fair standards, kissing them ;
Master Guitelmo offered him the keys
Of famine stricken Milan. All was naught "

VII

" Do you remember that sixth day of March ? "
Say^ Albert of Giussano : " he would have
The men-at-arms) the people, standards, all
Beneath his feet. From the three city gates
Forth came the people, came the battle-car
Prepared for war, the people cross in hand,
Before him the Carroccio's trumpets sound
Their last fanfare. The Carroccio's lofty mast
Before him bent, lowering the Gonfalon,
Until it swept the ground, he touched its hem.

VIII

" Do you remember ? Clad as penitents,"
Says Albert of Giussano, " bare-foot, cords
About our necks, our heads with ashes strewn.
We knelt in mire, with outstretched arms implored
For mercy. All there wept, the lords and knights
Who round him stood wept too, but he, upright
Upon his feet, beside th' Imperial shield.
In silence stood unmoved, looking on us
With that cold gaze of his, diamond keen.

IX

"Do you remember, on the morrow, how
Says Albert of Giussano, on the road
Returning to our shame, we saw behind
The gate the Empress gazing at us ? Then
We cast our crosses at her feet and cried
O fair, O pious Empress, lady true.
Have pity, pity on our women I She
Retired within and he on us imposed
That gates and walls be levelled to the ground.
So he with his embattled host might pass.

X

"Do you remember? Nine days did we wait,"
Says Albert of Giussano, " how Archbishop, counts,
With servile suite of vassals went away ;
The tenth day came the herald : ' Go ye forth
O wretched men, go forth and with you take
Your wives, your children and your goods. Eight days
The Emperor gives you.' ' Then with groans we ran
To Sant' Ambrogio, to the altars clung
And to the tombs. They chased us from the church.
Our wives, our little ones, like scurvy curs 1

XI

" Do you remember that Palm Sunday sad? "
Says Albert of Giussano. " Ah, that was
The passion of our Lord and of Milan !
From the four holy suburbs of our town
Three hundred towers of her encircling crown
We saw fall one by one ; then through the dust
Of ruins we beheld our houses razed,
Demolished, blasted ; files of skeletons
In some huge graveyard standing they appeared ;
Below, the bones still smouldered of our dead."

XII

Thus speaking Albert of Giussano raised
His two hands, covered up his eyes and wept.
There in the midmost of the Parliament
Like to a little child he sobbed and wept.
Then through the throng of all the Parliament
There ran a roar, as 'twere of savage beasts,
While from the doors and from the balconies
The women, pale, dishevelled, vnth their arms '
Outstretched, their wide dilated eyes turned towards
The Parliament, shrieked : " Kill the red-beard, kill I

XIII

" Behold," says Albert of Giussano, " Now
Behold I weep no more. Our day has come,
men of Milan, and we needs must win.
Behold, I dry mine eyes, and, looking up
To thee, O fair sun, shining in God's heaven,
I take an oath : To-morrow, ere the night.
Our dead in Purgatory shall hear good news
Which I myself will bear." — " Way," cry the people,
" To the Imperial heralds trust it rather"
Sinking 'neath Resegone smiled the sun.

Original text in Italian:

IL PARLAMENTO

"Della Canzone di Legnano, 1876-1879"

I

Sta Federico imperatore in Como.
Ed ecco un messaggero entra in Milano
Da Porta Nova a briglie abbandonate
« Popolo di Milano », ei passa e chiede,
« Fatemi scorta al console Gherardo ».
Il console era in mezzo de la piazza,
E il messagger piegato in su l'arcione
Parlò brevi parole e spronò via.
Allor fe' cenno il console Gherardo,
E squillaron le trombe a parlamento.

II

Squillarono le trombe a parlamento:
Ché non anche risurto era il palagio
Su' gran pilastri né l'arengo v'era,
Né torre v'era, né a la torre in cima
La campana. Fra i ruderi che neri
Verdeggiavan di spine, fra le basse
Case di legno, ne la breve piazza
I milanesi tenner parlamento
Al sol di maggio. Da finestre e porte
Le donne riguardavano e i fanciulli.

III

« Signori milanesi », il consol dice,
« La primavera in fior mena tedeschi
Pur come d'uso. Fanno pasqua i lurchi
Ne le lor tane, e poi calano a valle.
Per l'Engadina due scomunicati
Arcivescovi trassero lo sforzo.
Trasse la bionda imperatrice al sire
Il cuor fido e un esercito novello.
Como è co' i forti, e abbandonò la lega ».
il popol grida: « L'esterminio a Como! »

IV

« Signori milanesi », il consol dice,

« L'imperator, fatto lo stuolo in Como,

Move l'oste a raggiungere il marchese

Di Monferrato ed i pavesi. Quale

Volete, milanesi? od aspettare

Da l'argin novo riguardando in arme,

O mandar messi a Cesare, o affrontare

A lancia e spada il Barbarossa in campo? »

« A lancia e spada », tona il parlamento,

« A lancia e spada, il Barbarossa, in campo! »

V

Or si fa innanzi Alberto di Giussano.

Di ben tutta la spalla egli soverchia

Gli accolti in piedi al console d'intorno.

Ne la gran possa de la sua persona

Torreggia in mezzo al parlamento: ha in mano

La barbuta: la bruna capelliera

Il lato collo e l'ampie spalle inonda.

Batte il sol ne la chiara onesta faccia,

Ne le chiome e ne gli occhi risfavilla.

È la sua voce come tuon di maggio.

VI

« Milanesi, fratelli, popol mio!
Vi sovvien » dice Alberto di Giussano
« Calen di marzo? I consoli sparuti
Cavalcarono a Lodi, e con le spade
Nude in man gli giurâr l'obedienza.
Cavalcammo trecento al quarto giorno,
Ed a i piedi, baciando, gli ponemmo
I nostri belli trentasei stendardi.
Mastro Guitelmo gli offerì le chiavi
Di Milano affamata. E non fu nulla ».

VII

« Vi sovvien » dice Alberto di Giussano,
« Il dì sesto di marzo? A i piedi ei volle
Tutti i fanti ed il popolo e le insegne.
Gli abitanti venìan de le tre porte,
Il carroccio venìa parato a guerra;
Gran tratta poi di popolo, e le croci
Teneano in mano. Innanzi a lui le trombe
Del carroccio mandâr gli ultimi squilli,
Innanzi a lui l'antenna del carroccio
Inchinò il gonfalone. Ei toccò i lembi ».

VIII

« Vi sovvien? » dice Alberto di Giussano:
« Vestiti i sacchi de la penitenza,
Co' piedi scalzi, con le corde al collo,
Sparsi i capi di cenere, nel fango
C'inginocchiammo, e tendevam le braccia,
E chiamavam misericordia. Tutti
Lacrimavan, signori e cavalieri,
A lui d'intorno. Ei, dritto, in piedi, presso
Lo scudo imperial, ci riguardava,
Muto, co 'l suo diamantino sguardo ».

IX

« Vi sovvien » dice Alberto di Giussano,
« Che tornando a l'obbrobrio la dimane
Scorgemmo da la via l'imperatrice
Da i cancelli a guardarci? E pe' i cancelli
Noi gittammo le croci a lei gridando:
— O bionda, o bella imperatrice, o fida,
O pia, mercé, mercé di nostre donne! —
Ella trassesi indietro. Egli c'impose
Porte e muro atterrar de le due cinte
Tanto ch'ei con schierata oste passasse ».

X

« Vi sovvien? » dice Alberto di Giussano:
« Nove giorni aspettammo; e si partiro
L'arcivescovo i conti e i valvassori.
Venne al decimo il bando — Uscite, o tristi,
Con le donne, co' i figli e con le robe:
Otto giorni vi dà l'imperatore. —
E noi corremmo urlando a Sant'Ambrogio,
Ci abbracciammo a gli altari ed a i sepolcri.
Via da la chiesa, con le donne e i figli,
Via ci cacciaron come can tignosi ».

XI

« Vi sovvien », dice Alberto di Giussano,

« La domenica triste de gli ulivi?

Ahi passion di Cristo e di Milano!

Da i quattro Corpi santi ad una ad una

Crosciar vedemmo le trecento torri

De la cerchia; ed al fin per la ruina

Polverosa ci apparvero le case

Spezzate, smozzicate, sgretolate:

Parean file di scheltri in cimitero.

Di sotto, l'ossa ardean de' nostri morti ».

XII

Così dicendo Alberto di Giussano
Con tutt'e due le man copriasi gli occhi,
E singhiozzava: in mezzo al parlamento,
Singhiozzava e piangea come un fanciullo.
Ed allora per tutto il parlamento
Trascorse quasi un fremito di belve.
Da le porte le donne e da i veroni,
Pallide, scarmigliate, con le braccia
Tese e gli occhi sbarrati al parlamento
Urlavano — Uccidete il Barbarossa! —

XIII

« Or ecco », dice Alberto di Giussano,
« Ecco, io non piango più. Venne il dì nostro,
O milanesi, e vincere bisogna.
Ecco: io m'asciugo gli occhi, e a te guardando,
O bel sole di Dio, fo sacramento:
Diman da sera i nostri morti avranno
Una dolce novella in purgatorio:
E la rechi pur io! » Ma il popol dice:
« Fia meglio i messi imperiali ». Il sole
Ridea calando dietro il Resegone.

BIOGRAPHICAL NOTES

Giosuè Carducci
calen d' maggio 1880

Giosuè Carducci, (born July 27, 1835, Val di Castello, near Lucca, Tuscany [now Italy]—died Feb. 16, 1907, Bologna, Italy), Italian poet, winner of the Nobel Prize for Literature in 1906, and one of the most influential literary figures of his age.

The son of a republican country doctor, Carducci spent his childhood in the wild Maremma region of southern Tuscany. He studied at the University of Pisa and in 1860 became professor of Italian literature at Bologna, where he lectured for more than 40 years. He was made a senator for life in 1890 and was revered by the Italians as a national poet.

In his youth Carducci was the centre of a group of young men determined to overthrow the prevailing Romanticism and to return to classical models. Giuseppe Parini, Vincenzo Monti, and Ugo Foscolo were his masters, and their influence is evident in his first books of poems (Rime, 1857; later collected in Juvenilia [1880] and Levia gravia [1868; "Light and Serious Poems"]). Rime nuove (1887; The New Lyrics) and Odi barbare (1877; The Barbarian Odes) contain the best of Carducci's poetry: the evocations of the Maremma landscape and the memories of childhood; the lament for the loss of his only son; the representation of great historical events; and the ambitious attempts to recall the glory of Roman history and the pagan happiness of classical civilization. Carducci's enthusiasm for the classical in art led him to adapt Latin prosody to Italian verse, and his Odi barbare are written in metres imitative of Horace and Virgil. His research in Italian literature was warmed by his poetic imagination and style, and his best prose works equal his poetry.

Printed in Great Britain
by Amazon